RUNNING ON THE RAZOR'S EDGE: INDIA WITH NARENDRA MODI

DR. PHILIP K. JASSEN

To all my readers

Contents

Foreword

Modi with Nordic leaders

After India's decision to continue to buy oil from Russia, many experts of international relations have prophecised that India cannot take the pressure from USA or western world and would budge up necessarily. But India shows a tremendous skill on running on the rope, the recent visit of Modi to Europe has essentially proved it. Denmark, Finland, Germany, Japan, Quad have proved it that India is maturing rapidly and steadily. How this has become possible? How India has overcome the barrier?

Preface

From Nehru's ear to Indira's period and now the Modi age, India has seen many upheavels and torrents in its diplomatic relations and international affairs. But the latest developement after Russia's Ukraine invasion was perhaps a very tough challenge for Indian diplomacy. India's decision to continue to buy Russian crude oil is thought to impact India's relation with USA. But India, under Modi's leadership has been able to overcome it. His latest visit to Japan, Quad summit, Germany,Nordic countries has proved it.

Now it is to see how long India can maintain walking on the razor's edge?

Acknowledgements

All readers of international relations.

Prologue

Modi in Japan

India under prime minister Narendra Modi is somewhat different from other reigns. It is different. We have to study the subtle changes in policies to understand it.

After India's decision to continue to buy oil from Russia, many experts of international relations have prophecised that India cannot take the pressure from USA or western world and would budge up necessarily. But India shows a tremendous skill on running on the rope, the recent visit of Modi to Europe has essentially proved it. Denmark, Finland, Germany, Japan, Quad have proved it that India is maturing rapidly and steadily. How this has become possible? During his visit to Tokyo, Modi praised the foundation of IndiaJapan relations In the middle of his visit to Tokyo, Prime Minister Narendra Modi wrote an op-ed for Yomiuri Shimbun, one of Japan's five leading newspapers. In this report, Modi highlights India-Japan relations. The article was published on Monday, May 23. On Twitter, Prime Minister Modi shared the report, which was also published on the newspaper's website. He has written an article on the lively relations between India and Japan. We have a joint effort for peace, stability and prosperity. I look forward to the journey of our special friendship that marks 70 glorious years. " In the report, Prime Minister Modi described India-Japan relations as "special, strategic and global". "Cultural ties between the two countries date back many centuries," he said. The values of democracy, independence and confidence in the international system based on governance as well as the similarity of regional and international perspectives have brought the two countries closer to each other. The strong trust, confidence and genuine partnership between the two countries underpins the relationship between India and Japan. " From Bodhisena (an Indian monk who preached Buddhism in Japan in the Nara era) to Swami Vivekananda, cultural relations between the two countries are intertwined. They have a long and rich history of respect and learning, "he wrote. Modi said he believed in this partnership. Notably, when he was the Chief Minister of Gujarat, he praised the sophistication of Japanese technology and skills and recalled his long-term involvement in Japanese leadership and business. He writes that Japan has now become the preferred partner in Gujarat's industrial sector. Investment-Attracting Event - Vibrant Gujarat has also shown its most outstanding presence since its inception. "Japan has also proved that India is an unwavering partner in the process of development and modernization. From the automobile industry to industrial corridors, Japanese investment and development assistance extends across India. The high-speed rail project between Mumbai and Ahmedabad symbolizes Japan's broader cooperation in the most important endeavor towards a new India, "he wrote. During his two-day visit, Modi will hold bilateral meetings with Japanese Prime Minister Fumio Kishida, US President Joe Biden and newly elected Australian Prime Minister Anthony Albanese. In a tweet on Sunday evening, Prime Minister Modi said, "This evening, I am leaving for Japan to attend the second private Quad Summit. The quad leaders will again have the opportunity to discuss various quad initiatives and other issues of mutual interest. "

Stressing on India-Japan relations, Narendra Modi met three former prime ministers The three Japanese prime ministers met by Prime Minister Narendra Modi are Yoshihide Suga, Shinzo Abe and Yoshiro Mori. Prime Minister Narendra Modi is on a two-day visit to Japan. In a short span of time, he has met four current and former Prime Ministers of the country. Prime Minister Narendra Modi held a bilateral meeting with incumbent Japanese Prime Minister Fumio Kishidar in Tokyo on Tuesday. Earlier, he met with three former Japanese prime ministers. The three Japanese prime ministers met by Prime Minister Narendra Modi are Yoshihide Suga, Shinzo Abe and Yoshiro Mori. He congratulated the three former Japanese Prime Ministers on the development of India-Japan relations. As well as exchanged personal views with them. Tried to highlight personal chemistry. Yoshiro Mori is the current Chairperson of the Japan-India Association. Shinzo Abe will take over soon. This company was established in 1903. It is one of the oldest organizations in Japan. Prime Minister Modi has emphasized on further enhancing the political, economic and cultural ties between India and

Japan. So he also mentioned the special role of this organization. The Prime Minister wished Shinzo Abe well in his new role. He also appealed to the people to focus on maintaining friendly relations between the two countries. On the other hand, during the meeting with Sugar, the Prime Minister thanked him for further strengthening the bilateral relations between the two countries. They met in person at the first Quad Summit in Washington in 2021. With this, Prime Minister Narendra Modi joined the Quad Summit for the second time. The heads of state of Japan, Australia and the United States are also present at the event. Negotiations are underway to further enhance the strategic and global relations between the four countries. Prime Minister Modi is highlighting India's position there. Prime Minister Narendra Modi is on a two-day visit to Japan. He also attended a strategic meeting on Indo-Pacific region. After landing in Tokyo, he said the visit would provide him with opportunities to meet at the Quad Summit, meet fellow quad leaders, hold talks with Japanese business leaders and lively Indian leaders. He also addressed a meeting of expatriate Indians living in Japan. Talked to small children too.

CHAPTER TWO

Modi with Brics leaders

Quad has become an important place in front of the world in a very short time, Modi said at a conference in Japan Narendra Modi addressed the quad conference today. In his speech of about two and a half minutes in the first phase, he emphasized the importance of quads. However, Russia avoided the issue tactically. He emphasized the role of the Quad in its strategic position in the Indo-Pacific region. The Quad has become one of the most important alliances in the Indo-Pacific region. At the diplomatic level, both its necessity and importance have been equally placed before the world. And it has been in a very short time. This is what Prime Minister Narendra Modi said in his inaugural address at the Quad Conference. At the same time, he said, the quad has in fact set an example for democracies in the Indo-Pacific region. For which this alliance has played a fruitful role. The trust and cooperation of the quad member countries towards each other is inspiring a new initiative and new initiative among the flag-bearing states of democracy. In his remarks, Prime Minister Narendra Modi further said that the way in which the Quad member countries have enhanced mutual cooperation among themselves has created a spirit of mutual understanding and a liberating mindset and vision. Prime Minister Narendra Modi thinks that this is helping the growth of the quad. As a result, it is becoming easier to move forward with a specific goal in mind, he said. Besides, Prime Minister Modi lauded the way in which the quad member countries have cooperated with each other in tackling the Covid 19 epidemic. He also said that the role of member countries was very helpful especially with the Covid 19 vaccination. At the same time, he noted that the quad members are doing a very good job in dealing with climate change, following a simple method of exchanging goods between each other's countries, disaster management and interdependence of financial assistance. "Hopefully, this kind of cooperation and increased mutual awareness will further enrich the quad," he said. Modi also praised Australian Prime Minister Anthony Albanese. He said the way he joined the quad conference within 24 hours of being sworn in as Australian prime minister was truly commendable. Modi also congratulated Albany for this. With that said, Albanese's activism proves how sincere and responsible the Australian Quad is about the future. Prime Minister Modi has left for Tokyo on a two-day visit to attend a quad conference at the invitation of Japanese Prime Minister Fumio Kishida. This is the third conference of the quad. In addition to the Prime Minister of India, the quad conference was attended by US President Joe Biden and the Prime Minister of Australia Anthony Albanese. Basically, the quad has been made up of 4 countries. These are Japan, India, America and Australia. The alliance has also been labeled an Asian NATO by the international diplomatic community.

CHAPTER THREE

Modi at pashupatinath

Recently China has tried very seriously to woo Nepal and thus creating tension between India and Nepal. Modi's latest visit has somewhat mitigated the smoke.

Prime Minister Modi will visit Lumbini, Nepal on the occasion of Buddhapurnima, with the aim of strengthening relations between the two countries He was very keen to take part in the worship at the Mayadevi temple on the occasion of the holy Buddha Jayanti. He also said that he was very honored to have the opportunity to pay homage to the holy birthplace of Lord Buddha like millions of Indians. Prime Minister Narendra Modi will visit Nepal on Buddhapurnima tomorrow (May 16) at the invitation of Nepal's Prime Minister Sher Bahadur Deuba. Baribar said that himself. He said he would go to Lumbini, Nepal. He said he was keen to take part in worship at the Mayadevi temple on the occasion of the holy Buddha Jayanti. He also said that he was very honored to have the opportunity to pay homage to the holy birthplace of Lord Buddha like millions of Indians. The Prime Minister of Nepal visited India last month. At that time, the two of them discussed several issues. He also said that it was very fruitful. He also said that the Prime Minister is very optimistic about the meeting with Prime Minister Deuba once again. Prime Minister Narendra Modi also said that the two countries would continue to work together to enhance cooperation in various fields including hydropower, development and communication. Modi said that besides visiting the holy Mayadevi temple, he would also attend the groundbreaking ceremony of the India International Center for Buddhist Culture and Heritage at Lumbini Math. He will also take part in a function organized by the Government of Nepal on the occasion of Buddha Jayanti. India's relationship with Nepal is beautiful and strong. Civilizations and people-to-people contacts between India and Nepal provide a lasting foundation for the close ties between the two countries. The purpose of his visit is to celebrate and strengthen the ties between the two countries which have become stronger with time. He said the relationship between the two countries had developed over the centuries and was recorded in the long history of interaction between the two countries. Tomorrow is Buddhapurnima. The day is observed with reverence all over the country. Buddha's words are remembered on this day as well as the rituals of worship. Gautama Buddha preached the message of peace and harmony. The religion ideology he preached hundreds of years ago is still relevant. Like India, Gautam Buddha is remembered in Nepal. He was born into a royal family in this country. Then he left the family and pursued. He also achieves success. Only then does he propagate his own ideology. He has countless fans in India, Nepal and China.

Modi and Macron

Macron welcomes Narendra Modi to France, talks on Russian aggression Foreign Ministry spokesperson Arindam Bagchi said that Prime Minister Narendra Modi has arrived in France. Last week, Macron was re-elected president. The foreign ministry also said the two leaders would hold a strategic meeting. Prime Minister Narendra Modi arrived in France on Wednesday on the last leg of his three day European tour. He will speak with French President Emmanuel Macron. This is the first time a foreign head of state has visited France since being elected French president for the second time. In Paris, the capital of France, Prime Minister Narendra Modi tweeted that France is one of India's strongest allies. Mutual cooperation between the two countries will be further enhanced. Foreign Ministry spokesperson Arindam Bagchi said that Prime Minister Narendra Modi has arrived in France. Last week, Macron was re-elected president. The foreign ministry also said the two leaders would hold a strategic meeting. There will be talks on strengthening bilateral relations and trade relations between the two countries. This year marks the 65th year of diplomatic relations between India and France. This is Narendra Modi's fifth visit to France during his two terms as Prime Minister. French President Macron had earlier visited India in 2016. According to sources, Emanuele Macron can talk with Prime Minister Narendra Modi about Russia's aggression in Ukraine. He has hosted a dinner. There may also be pressure to remove Russia's ambassador to India. However, just as India has signed multiple military agreements with France, it also has multiple agreements with Russia. The Prime Minister was welcomed by the Indians in Paris. The Prime Minister left for Europe on Monday. He arrived in France, first in Germany, then in Denmark. The Prime Minister will return to the country from here. On the first day of his visit to Europe, Prime Minister Narendra Modi addressed the Indians in Ballirne, Germany. There, he said, in 2021, 40 percent of the total real-time digital paint in the world was in India. He also highlighted his government's efforts to integrate technology users with the administration. Talking about India's success in the visit, he invited German businessmen to invest in the country. Addressing the Indians, Prime Minister Narendra Modi said, "The way technology is being used with the administration in India has created a new India." However, while talking about this, he sneered at the opposition Congress. "There are a number of services being offered online in India at present," he said. As a result, there is no need to tell any Prime Minister that I send one rupee from Delhi and only 15 paise goes to the people. The Prime Minister stood up in Germany and asked what kind of 'hand' was there before that 75 paise did not reach the common man? The Prime Minister said that now the Government of India is providing about 10,000 services online. As a result, everything from farmers to government assistance, to scholarships, is being paid directly. The money is going directly to the bank accounts of the consumers

Courtesy of friendship, Danish Prime Minister shows Modi around her home

Modi with Danish prime minister

Courtesy of friendship, Danish Prime Minister shows Modi around her home On the same day, Prime Minister Narendra Modi addressed a joint press conference with Danish Prime Minister Mate Fredericksen. In Denmark, Prime Minister Modi said, "We have called for an immediate ceasefire in Ukraine." India and Denmark. These two countries created new patterns of friendship. Courtesy of Prime Minister Narendra Modi's visit to Denmark. Modi arrives in Denmark on Tuesday for the second leg of his European tour. At the Copenhagen airport, Prime Minister Modi was welcomed by Danish Prime Minister Mate Fredericksen. On this day, Mete Frederickson invited Prime Minister Narendra Modi to his residence. Show the whole house. During his visit to India, Modi presented Frederickson with a painting of Orissa. He also showed his memories on this day. It has been reported that Narendra Modi may attend the second India Nordic Summit. On the same day, Prime Minister Narendra Modi addressed a joint press conference with Danish Prime Minister Mate Fredericksen. In Denmark, Prime Minister Modi said, "We have called for an immediate ceasefire in Ukraine." He was speaking at a news conference after arriving in Denmark as part of the second leg of a three-nation tour of Europe. During the Virtual Summit between Modi and Danish Prime Minister Mate Fredericksen in September 2020, bilateral relations reached the level of "Green Strategic Partnership". Frederickson visited India from 9 to 11 October 2021. Meanwhile, at the India-Germany bilateral meeting on Monday, Berlin called New Delhi its super partner. Modi held bilateral talks with Federal Chancellor Olaf Schulz in Berlin on Monday. The two leaders co-chaired the sixth edition of the Indo-German Intergovernmental Consultation (IGC). The biennial IGC is a different kind of negotiating platform, featuring pictures of bilateral talks between leaders of different states. It is to be noted that this is the first IGC discussion of the Prime Minister with Chancellor Scholes. It is also the first government-to-government discussion of the new German government. In December 2021, Chancellor Scholes officially took office. The German administration has said that they are quite optimistic about Narendra Modi's visit. The two leaders held a press briefing after meeting Prime Minister Modi. On behalf of Germany, Chancellor Schulz said, "Economically, India is a super partner for Germany in Asia in terms of security policy and climate political terms." Germany added: "India is one of our most important partners here. Development is possible only when every country in the world, not just a handful of countries, is an equal partner in that development. India believes in this belief just like Germany. "

CHAPTER SIX

Germany pledges 10 billion euros for green, financial aid to India On Monday, Prime Minister Narendra Modi and German Chancellor Wolf Schulz issued a joint statement on the two countries' partnership in green hydrogen. They said, two countries. 'Indo-German Green Hydrogen Roadmap. India and Germany have signed an agreement on the Green Project. Due to this project, Germany will provide 10 billion Euros for greening and development projects to India by 2030. India and Germany made the announcement at a joint press conference. At a press conference at the end of the first leg of Prime Minister

Narendra Modi's visit to Europe on Monday, Indian Foreign Secretary Binoy Quatra said that Joint Director Intent had given a long-term strategic vision to the development cooperation agenda between India and Germany. This communication will be taken further. He added that as part of the project, Germany would provide 10 billion euros in financial assistance to India by 2030. The Foreign Secretary further said that an agreement has been signed between the two countries for cooperation on green hydrogen and renewable issues. In this case India will build a green hydrogen hub with the help of a tax force German as part of India's partnership. On Monday, Prime Minister Narendra Modi and German Chancellor Wolf Schulz issued a joint statement on the two countries' partnership in green hydrogen. They said, two countries. 'Indo-German Green Hydrogen Roadmap. The Indo-German Energy Forum will also set up a tax force to look into the matter. About nine agreements were signed between the two countries on Monday on the occasion of the sixth Indo-German government consultation. The Prime Minister was in Germany on the first day of his three-day visit to Europe. From there, Modi's destination is Denmark. Finally, the Prime Minister will return home from France. Modi received the official guard of honor after a bilateral meeting with German Chancellor Olaf Schulz. Scholes took over as German Chancellor in December 2021. Then this was Modi's first visit to Germany. Addressing the Indians, the Prime Minister said, "This is the same country that you were forced to leave this country for a while. There is that bureaucracy, there is that office, there is paper and pen. But the results are much better now than before. On the same day, Prime Minister Narendra Modi highlighted the success of Direct Benefit Transfer Schemes. He said that through this scheme large sums are going to be sent to the consumers.

CHAPTER SEVEN

'Germany's Super Partner India', Narendra Modi won the hearts of Berlin during the tour Prime Minister Narendra Modi was invited to Germany as a guest at the G7 summit in late June. During his visit, an official guard of honor was given on the arrival of Prime Minister Modi. Modi won the heart of Europe. In his first foreign tour in 2022, he visited Germany and established India at a new height. On May 2, the Prime Minister visited Germany, Denmark and France. Germany is a very old friend of India.

It's like rekindling that relationship. It is especially important for India to have this old friend by its side during the war in Russia and Ukraine, two more European countries. Modi did the work of that catalyst. At the India-Germany bilateral meeting, Berlin called New Delhi its super partner. Modi held bilateral talks with Federal Chancellor Olaf Schulz in Berlin on Monday. The two leaders co-chaired the sixth edition of the IndoGerman Intergovernmental Consultation (IGC). The biennial IGC is a different kind of negotiating platform, featuring pictures of bilateral talks between leaders of different states. It is to be noted that this discussion is going to be the first IGC of the Prime Minister with Chancellor Scholes. It is also the first government-to-government discussion of the new German government. In December 2021, Chancellor Scholes officially took office. The German administration has said that they are quite optimistic about Narendra Modi's visit. The two leaders held a press briefing after meeting Prime Minister Modi. On behalf of Germany, Chancellor Schulz said, "Economically, India is a super partner for Germany in Asia in terms of security policy and climate-political terms." Germany added: "India is one of our most important partners here. Development is possible only when every country in the world, not just a handful of countries, is an equal partner in that development. India believes in this belief just like Germany. " Talking about Germany's special relationship with India, the Chancellor said he was glad to have the first intergovernmental talks of his administration with the Indian government. The Chancellor further said, "We are pleased that this Government has held its first intergovernmental talks with the Government of India. To me, it sets a special precedent for relations between the two countries. " On the same day,

Prime Minister Narendra Modi was invited to Germany as a guest at the G7 summit in late June. During his visit, an official guard of honor was given on the arrival of Prime Minister Modi. During his three-day visit, Prime Minister Modi is scheduled to travel to Denmark on Tuesday for talks with Nordic leaders.